One Million Tiny Cuts

One Million Tiny Cuts

Matt Duggan

Clare Songbirds
Publishing House

Clare Songbirds Publishing House Chapbook Series
ISBN 978-1-947653-08-5

One Million Tiny Cuts© 2017 Matt Duggan
All Rights Reserved. Clare Songbirds Publishing House retains
right to reprint.
Permission to reprint individual poems must be obtained from
the author who owns the copyright.

Printed in the United States of America
FIRST EDITION

Clare Songbirds Publishing House
140 Cottage Street
Auburn, New York 13021
www.ClareSongbirdspub.com

Contents

Monster	1
Let My Blood always be part of Europe	2
Reality	3
El Contentiones Stint	4
Empty Rooms	5
One Million Tiny Cuts	6
In the Belly of Massachusetts	7
Slipping Away from the Radar	8
The Spaces Left Bare	9
Drinking with Hemingway	10
House of Spikes	11
Aspects of Integrity	12
The Glass man	13
Feeding	14
Diary of Water	15
The Echo Chamber	16
The Blooming	17
Hinterland	18
A Portrait of Park Benches	19
Ithaki	20

Acknowlegements

"House of Spikes" first published in *Osiris*

"Ithaki" first published in *The Dawntreader*

"The Echo Chamber" first published in *Algebra of Owls*

"Diary of Water" first published by *Ink, Sweat, and Tears*

"Spaces Left Bare" first appeared in *Proletarian Poetry*

"Drinking with Hemingway" first published by *Midnight Lane Boutique* also filmed for the *Poets with a View* documentary by Omir Lior.

"The Feeding" appeared in *Anapest Journal*

"The Glass Man" published in *The Orson's Review* and *The Journal*

"In the Belly of Massachusetts" published in *The Journal*

"One Million Tiny Cuts" and "Portrait of Park Benches"
appeared in *Anti Heroin Chic Journal*

This book is dedicated to the love of my life Kelly Thomas for supporting me and sticking by me through hard times and good, and for all the poets and writers who have supported my event 'Poetry in the Pond' over the last couple of years, you know who you are.

Monster

Faces of such beauty
hide the monster within
throwing sunflower head's
nine inch nails sewn into their stems.

I, the metal parts
white bones engaged in the enemy,
fists have become open wounds
where blood pours like a fountain of violets;

dripping from the sole of angels
who smoke cigarettes outside crematoriums,
I can't help the tongue and its lacerations
slowly healing from ululating giants;

Whose flesh I see cold and wooden
as frozen and chipped sycamore.
In time I will see them as only dishonest children
hopscotching in a sea of rumours and chains.

Let my Blood always be part of Europe

Take my hand and guide me through the streets
where circles appear in espresso cups
shop windows are decorated
in red chorizo beside hairy legs of lamb.

Let me breathe inside
the remaining arm of La Maquita
brush shoulders with the turquoise giants of Berlin
run through the dark valley of Venetian side streets;

Sip Aperol Spritz
while watching water circle the oak bricole.
Let my blood always be part of Europe

my skin the land that I so endure,
take my hand and make me walk these streets again,
a love affair without a cure.

Reality

I want to walk in the air smell lavender and cigarette fumes
talk with the citizens share stories of debt and woe;
feel the summer breath whispering on my neck
live in a world where not everything ends with an emoji.

Take away these toys let me walk in the real world
where I can see my enemies from afar;
not the cowards hidden behind computer screens
who mark my back with a one thousand tiny scars.

I want to live in a world
where not everything ends with an emoji.

Et Contentiones Stint

I see the covetous nature of all that they expect
weaving in life like dirty water
that surrounds a dying rose,
beyond shallow ground hooks of envious fatalism
swing their torso backwards where my endurance
has reached its final boiling point.

I try to hide the pumping brown veins
that have ripped into a shade of carmine,
where the idiocy of their selfish ambitions
crawls inside my eyes like crestfallen worms,
when does that thief of flattery become the salient enemy
that you selflessly mould.

They will take the blood of goodwill
place it inside a transparent bayonet which you cannot see,
when time allows you will smell the scent of enmity
their parody will end as an endless reflection
held inside a whale's head
the sperm on a cracked bathroom mirror
that wavers at the bottom of the sea.

Empty Rooms

Safety is a wall that has character
between grey crevice thin plasterboard,
I hear the voice that have become my family,
they do not know that I regard them as such
it's only when we pass that we acknowledge each other
a smile or a nod that gives me the recognition
that I am still part of the human race.
Yet I live in empty rooms listening to the dust mites
the ornamental catfish that hides my isolation,
in a world that has severed me from conversation and touch.

One Million Tiny Cuts

How did you cope with the first tiny cut?
the milk that drained from the soul.
Did that cut lay inscribed on your back?
how did the mechanism work for you.

Some never reveal their first tiny cut
thin tissue that departed into liquid,
shrugged as a learning curve of emotions
while other's build a solid resistance;

killing sorrow before it spreads into their blood
age will always teach us the value
in the cracks that will reappear,

as they do not see the one million tiny cuts
embellished on your back which strengthens resolve,
in a battlefield where you feed on another tiny cut.

In The Belly of Massachusetts

Lungs - giant tanks of iron
skyline gathered in cement tracers
traffic lights hovered in metallic yellow huts
above freeways that swerve and breathe,
like obese concrete circles of eight.
The Liver a swinging hinge
hanging from a waterfall where dead coats of seahorses
danced with dehydrated salmon skins.
Along sidewalks where veterans with no legs
jibe for dollar bits among the shaking junkies
where cuts of beef as large as window frames
simmered on plates of plastic gold.

Slipping Away from the Radar

Feeling the urge to slip away from the radar
Seek isolation from the jarred voices
that hook raindrops from autumn skies,
a lingering presence
leeches sucking on the human soul.
I'd like to leave my car keys dangling
like Weldon Kee's with just a beautiful view,
rest well on Robinson's Bench

where the digging blades no longer spike inside the spine
an anatomy of manipulation would remain with the vipers

snapping at my heels,

on a far- away shoreline that no one could reach.

The Spaces Left Bare

The only human figures to pass on these walls
are the shadows in opposing rooms
those reflections
during the summer months
bounce from the ceiling like ghosts dressed in black suits.

Air is stale and needs recycling
windows gleam with no visible fingerprints,
immaculate laminated tiles

underfloor heating
the spaces are left bare. ......
...
.

Where beneath the plush gothic balcony
a homeless man sleeps in the open air
at night the room lights up for no one
then fades as dusk wakes the clock;
where guests will never reserve or stay.

Drinking with Hemingway

Break the midnight
when the summer chrome melts into a cacophony of voices,
where neon alley ways smell of cigarettes and cooked
lemon grass.

Dealers with oxycontin smiles
street walkers tout the same space that their great ancestors
once paced for their very own pleasure seeking,

enter into a bar that looks like a brothel
with the curtains drawn
where cocaine is exchanged in palms outside
and the whores are busy sweating in doorways
and local hotels.

I felt a oneness with Hemingway
after my fourteenth sip of absinthe,
the wallpaper a cabinet of empty green bottles
ceiling peeling in dark mahogany as a swinging chande-
lier turns black and white.

The many faces add colours to the room,
come break the midnight with me
watch the vessels clamber to madness,
see what he saw from these tables in blood bleached oak.

House of Spikes

In circles the streets swerve
Under light hidden away;
I catch the shadow of Catalonia
See ghosts in emerald uniforms
Against palm trees where abstract graffiti
Only warm the brass begging bowls.
Yellow flags brush in airy spectrum
Hanging from balconies where dirty washing
sways with blue stars. I rest close by the gothic cathedral
this Faustian house of spikes –
sipping green drinks with sugar and spoon,
listening to the language that hangs in skies
like the sound of ocean choking on missing words.

Written in Barcelona after visiting Sagrada Familia

Aspects of Integrity

I am that single blade of grass
remains of selfless integrity,
surrounded by thirsty claws
weaving inside rustic machinery,

clipping the quarry of my dreams
I am not a prisoner anymore
Not a follower of crowd pleasing algorithm,

sucked dry by the lickspittle
arched in the trending prisms
slaved by the utopian measures
that I should be forced to like,

I am that single blade of grass
that stands tall against cloned towers
a gorging fist eager to rip out
the guts of ink shielded cronyism,
I am that single blade of grass.

The Glass Man

A tired man made of glass
wakes from his unmade bed
we see into his life through his transparent skin,
a witness to all the tears
he gathers and sheds.
We see every day what's inside this glass man's head

hourly notifications
on his banal and meaningless life
thoughts and desperation of a man wanting to be liked,
We watch the cracks a glass man
wandering the clockworks of his mind
we watch and can almost write
what the glass man is thinking,

What saturates the skin
from the blood that's written in the sand?
A tired man made of glass turns to a world
where everyone has chipped away a piece of him
held the same mirror to their own lives,
believing that no one else would see his reflection

The Feeding

It was only on an august evening
when the clouds were as black as clockwork
sky grey with one pumping vein
shaking the occasional raindrop,
that I noticed and could see
the animals chewing on my flesh,
(I once hunted and joked with them.)

When they think that you are done
a relic with wounds used for their own sickly delectation,
they   *feed*
feed
Feed

Leaving a slight beat
a bare bone
I, weak, still have a flame burning in the pit of my eye
thinking phoenix in my stomach,
waiting for that perfect moment when I will rise once again
start *feeding* on their flesh for the very last time.

Diary of Water

We rise from the water
tunnels spinning from seabed,
our first pierced breaths of oxygen
are like an embryonic rush for birth
swaying on the surface –
half in one world - breath and sight in another.
We reached the barrens of land
through countless incarnations of various deities
we had come out of the water
surviving on the land
knowing we were always sea-bound
a curse for the mother of the gods.
We would return to the oceans
when concrete flames in a strawberry moon
Burning flags and prophesy
Will we once again be the liquid before birth
the after flood after death,
Ink in a diary of water.

The Echo Chamber

Every night I listen to a man going mad
it starts with the moving of wardrobes
the wincing cry through thin plasterboard
a building crescendo of expletives;

repeated again and again at the voices that surround him,
every night I listen to a man going mad
until one night the screams were paused
no sound of friction behind his thin walls;

just rolling sirens melting in the windows raindrops
that blue and red repetition,
as they escort his spirit from the bedroom
where a blister pack of pills lay untouched.

The Blooming

A white petal among a meadow of monochrome salutes;
it's stem half clipped
scattered in cold season of fascism.
Ink from the righteous
poured on silent red -
                                      Words
defining the acts of the voiceless;
Only lips too scared would pluck the only white rose.

This rose has no head
time would harvest the blooming;
Each silent rose replaced by the purest;
When one hundred petals of white
fell at our feet
on this fine, sunny day,
                                  Where she had to go;
A white petal
among a meadow of monochrome salutes.

Written for the 71st anniversary of the execution of Sophie Scholl, an Anti-Nazi political activist who was one of the founding members of 'The White Rose' a non-violent resistant group in Nazi Germany.

Hinterland

Walk in my Hinterland breathe through straws of sun,
Step on the cobbled grey
where angels stalk the perimeter of day.

Gaze towards phallic tubes
smoking death,
through red concrete a glittery coat -

where Seagulls feed on a circled shaped crow
like roadkill in blackened slate
far from broken waves that pulsate the blood of the land.

Humming green arena – these whispers of motorway;
Just punch marks in plasterboard
Decorated like holy bullet holes.

I drift in the light where sea chains shackled to the harbour;
Sway me into openings of yellow reflections
Like a sea otter counting fish heads – Walk with me in my Hinterland.

A Portrait of Park Benches

Summer evening in June
a square field in short embers
long emerald –
frozen crow like miniature statue in coal
blood trees
shake nervous leaves from their bones,
falling like bullets
shaped as acorns into streams.

The only requiem I see these days
are the silver and blue plaques
etched into the centre of park benches,
no place of birth or worship -
wasteland in camera and scarlet ruin.

Ithaki

I.
Trojan bronze and coin embedded in Ionian turquoise blue;
where metal black crows span above a man spraying spittle
over weaved baskets in strips of long bamboo - skinned.
I suckled on Tzatziki and lamb Kleftiko
consumed a carafe of Grecian wine;
saw the stars of Ithaca dance with mountain songs
bells chimed like the after-dinner shrill from deranged sirens.
Gazed like the God's at amber and crystal blue boxes
jarred along a shark bitten tail shaped bay
prickled fruit – decaying pomegranate
peeling red flesh inside the opened draining of day.
I travelled on the navy blue albatross
wooden fin splicing through Hellenic water; Triangles in
translucent green
reflections from the feverish and mad
the faces of those who had come before me.

II.
Half sunken Byzantium shaped ships
moulded into yellow cliff - Crescendo of beach crickets surfing
on the sound buckles of Poseidon wrists,
I swam in the strong currents – mangled in storms
Tumbling through rotten ship masts
lined with dead pine trees; My lungs filled with salt
while white snappers nibbled at my blue flesh,
my limp body awakened and dragged to the surface of a
unfamiliar sea.
A beautiful woman with olive skin and tarantula coloured
hair held me
I peered down into the depths of clear ocean,
noticing she had dolphin heads as human feet
her complexion and breasts as smooth as soft whale skin;
In an ancient tongue she pointed to the rise of sun
a pink centre of valley - shining marble from the caves of
the nymph;
as I swam closer I saw the chipped face of Odyssey
shaped in the marbled mountain
in green cypress print – Inside the cave Penelope weaved
her twenty first shroud.

Matt Duggan is a Bristol born poet his work has appeared in many journals such as *Osiris, The Journal, Ink, Sweat, and Tears, Harbinger Asylum, Apogee Magazine, Algebra of Owls, Midnight Lane Boutique, Prole, The Fat Damsel, Into the Void, Carillon, The Orson's Review, Anapest Journal, Black Light Engine Room, Laldy Literary Journal, Graffiti,* and many others.

In 2015 Matt won the prestigious erbacce prize for poetry with his first full collection *Dystopia 38.10* and read from his collection at many venues in the U.K. Matt has also read internationally on the island of Paxos, in Greece and was invited to read at The Poetry on the Lakes Festival in Orta, Italy. In 2016 he won the *Into the Void Poetry Prize* with his poem "Elegy for Magdalene" and was invited to read at the Luminous Echoes Event in Boston in 2017. Matt also became one of six core members at erbacce-press where he supports new poets to the press and reads with the other members for the erbacce prize.

Matt will be reading from this new collection, *One Million*

Tiny Cuts, at London's The Poetry Café in October, 2017. He is also involved in a new documentary project called *Poems with a View* which is a new project produced and filmed by Omri Lior, an Israeli film maker, the project consists of short film clips showing eminent poets of different nationalities reading their own work.

Matt has been invited back to read in Boston for the Poetry Reading Series at Cambridge Public Library in April 2018. He will also be doing his first readings in New York for The Greater Weather for Media event at The Parkside Lounge, followed by another reading at Sip This with Peter V. Dugan and George Wallace.

www.ingramcontent.com/pod-product-compliance
Lightning Source LLC
Chambersburg PA
CBHW010408130526
44592CB00050B/2661